presented to: _____

from: _____

THE
Twenty-Third
Psalm

for the
Brokenhearted

THE
TWENTY-THIRD
Psalm

~for the~
Brokenhearted

CARMEN LEAL

ISBN 0-89957-160-3

First printing—September 2005

Cover designed by Market Street Design, Inc., Chattanooga, Tennessee
Interior design and typesetting by The Livingstone Corporation, Carol Stream, Illinois
Edited and proofread by Agnes Lawless, Dan Penwell, The Livingstone Corporation, Donna Clark Goodrich, and Rick Steele.

Printed in Italy

11 10 09 08 07 06 05–L–8 7 6 5 4 3 2 1

To my sister, Diane. You are
a beautiful woman—inside and out.
Your strength, courage, and your
faith in the Shepherd will heal
your broken heart.

Contents

Introduction

I KNOW THE SHEPHERD

A Shakespearean actor of great fame was known for his ability to breathe life into the classics. He routinely performed his one-man show of renowned literature to packed houses, his resonant voice filling the auditorium. After thrilling his audiences with dozens of versatile selections, he ended his performance with a dramatic reading of Psalm 23. For years this beloved passage, the *pièce de résistance*, brought audiences to their feet, thunderous applause accompanying the actor's deep bows.

One night as the acclaimed thespian prepared to recite Psalm 23, a young man in the front row stood and asked permission to speak. The crowd was horrified at the interruption, but the gracious actor invited him to say what was on his mind.

"Please sir," said the younger man in a small voice, "I know you always complete your

You will seek me and find me when you seek me with all your heart.
—Jeremiah 29:13

performance with Psalm 23, but I wonder if I might recite it instead?"

Gasps and murmurs filled the auditorium. *How dare an insignificant, untrained youth think he could compete with such magnificent talent?* The actor was surprised by this unusual request, but curiosity prompted him to invite the man to come forward.

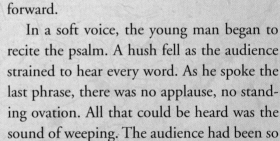

In a soft voice, the young man began to recite the psalm. A hush fell as the audience strained to hear every word. As he spoke the last phrase, there was no applause, no standing ovation. All that could be heard was the sound of weeping. The audience had been so moved by the young man's recitation that every eye was full of tears.

"I don't understand," the puzzled actor said to the youth. "I have been performing Psalm 23 for years, yet I have never been able to move an audience as you have tonight. I trained at Julliard. I won an Academy Award and have played before kings and presidents. You're nothing more than a boy. What is your secret?"

The young man humbly replied, "Well sir, you know the psalm . . . but I know the Shepherd."

Henri Nouwen was right when he said, "Our life is full of brokenness—broken relationships, broken promises, broken expectations. How can we live with that brokenness without becoming bitter and resentful except by returning again and again to God's faithful presence in our lives?" No one is exempt from brokenness. Whether your heart is broken from the end of a marriage, the loss of a friend, the death of a pet, or the myriad of hurts that come our way, remember that the Shepherd wants to comfort you.

Knowing the Shepherd is much more important than knowing the psalm, but knowing the psalm can help you know the Shepherd. The stories in

The Twenty-Third Psalm for the Brokenhearted show us that this passage is as relevant and comforting to us today as it was to David when he penned the words. This book is filled with examples of people who have learned that God can heal broken hearts, but you have to give every piece to the Shepherd of the brokenhearted.

I would rather walk with God in the dark than go alone in the light.
—Mary Gardiner Brainard

INTRODUCTION

The LORD is my shepherd, I shall not be in want.
He makes me lie down in green pastures,
he leads me beside quiet waters, he restores my soul.
He guides me in paths of righteousness for his name's sake.
Even though I walk through the valley of the shadow of death,
I will fear no evil, for you are with me;
your rod and your staff, they comfort me.
You prepare a table before me in the presence of my enemies.
You anoint my head with oil; my cup overflows.
Surely goodness and love will follow me all the days of my life,
and I will dwell in the house of the LORD forever.

PSALM 23

CHAPTER ONE

THE
SHEPHERD WHO
Cares

"THE LORD IS MY SHEPHERD"

TRUST HIS HEART

Only the Shepherd knew when David would die. Hospice said that he wouldn't be here on Christmas, and it broke my heart. But even hospice was surprised at how quickly the end came. This had been an excruciatingly long road. At times I begged for his and my release from this illness that destroyed his body, his brain, and our dreams.

After vowing never to trust another man when my heart was broken in a devastating way, I met David. We walked past a florist shop one day, and he commented on the gorgeous bouquet of red roses in the window.

Cast all your anxiety on him because he cares for you.
—1 Peter 5:7

"Red roses are what a husband gives to a wife when he's been cheating on her," I told him. "I hate red roses."

David stroked my hand, gave it a squeeze, and we continued our walk. Later, after he knew that I was "the one," he had flowers delivered. When I came home from work that day a magnificent arrangement of yellow roses was on the coffee table. "I'll never give you a reason to receive red roses," read the card. That was the day I knew I could trust David.

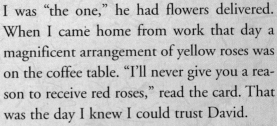

As we planned the wedding, we went through counseling with our pastor. He asked both of us our greatest fear in getting married, and I knew the answer right away. My fear was that David would get sick, and I'd have to be his caregiver. I really do not like being anywhere near sick people. I voiced my concern, and David shared his, and the session continued. I knew I could trust this man to stick around forever and that our marriage would grow stronger each day. But that's not exactly what happened.

On our third wedding anniversary, David learned that his forgetfulness, weight loss, falls, and odd behavior for the previous eighteen months weren't due to stress. No restful cruise or sessions with a counselor would bring back the man I had fallen in love with and married. I'd never heard of Huntington's disease before that life-changing evening when David came in from seeing a neurologist, but reading the brief entry in the encyclopedia caused my heart to shatter into what felt like a hundred fragments.

Two weeks later, I still couldn't stop crying. Despite the music from our annual Christmas cantata playing in my kitchen, I didn't have a single shred of excitement or joy in my life. *It isn't supposed to be like this,* I thought hitting the off button to stop the music.

Before me, even as behind, God is, and all is well.
—John Greenleaf Whittier

"God, what were you thinking?" I cried as I ripped the cassette out and threw it against the wall. "You knew this was going to happen. You know I hate being around sick people. David's not only sick, he's terminal, and it's all your fault!" I knew yelling at God wouldn't help, but expressing my anger felt good.

Over the next six weeks, I learned about the disease that was killing my husband. With each piece of information, I found another reason not to trust the Shepherd. Still, I learned the music for the cantata, went to rehearsal, and, gradually, a strange thing happened.

Music is said to be the speech of angels, according to Thomas Carlyle. He wasn't talking specifically about the program we rehearsed that Christmas, but, in the midst of my heartache, the angels spoke through one specific song.

In the beginning, every word, every note of Babbie Mason singing *Trust His Heart* was like a heel smashing the fragile shards of my splintered heart. I didn't understand, I didn't know his plan, and I didn't want to know it if it meant losing my husband. I didn't want to trust his heart.

But as I sang about a God who was too good to be unkind, to wise to make mistakes, the words pierced through my misery. At times I felt that no one understood or cared about me, but then I'd sing about struggles that make it impossible to see the truth, and I remembered that the Shepherd cared. Shortly before Christmas, the words became, not the personal attack they seemed that first day, but a cherished message delivered by the angels.

David is singing in the heavenly choir this Christmas. Over the years, I have had to trust the Shepherd and his plan for my life. One day I sat next to David and listened to his labored breathing. As my tears splashed, I held his hand and sang to him. I told him that it was okay to be scared, to wonder why things were happening, but all he had to do was to trust. More than any other song, this one has helped me remember that the Shepherd does care. All I have to do is trust his heart.

May the God of hope fill you with all joy and peace as you trust in him, so that you may overflow with hope by the power of the Holy Spirit.
—Romans 15:13

God loves each of us as if there were only one of us.
—St. Augustine

I NEED THEE EVERY HOUR

ANNIE S. HAWKS

I need Thee ev'ry hour, Most gracious Lord;

No tender voice like Thine Can peace afford.

I need Thee; oh, I need Thee!

Ev'ry hour I need Thee!

Oh, bless me now, my Savior;

I come to Thee

CHAPTER TWO

THE
SHEPHERD WHO
Provides

"I SHALL NOT BE IN WANT"

SOMETHING BETTER

It started like any end-of-the-year meeting with the principal going over anticipated changes for the next school term. But as he assigned classrooms and discussed who would teach what grade level, Janet realized her name had not been mentioned. Without a word, her eyes suddenly tearing, she stood and left the room.

Janet's stress level rose as she drove home after learning the news. Why was her position eliminated? What was going to happen to her family? Her husband, Craig, a California rancher, was swamped with land and equipment bills. With four children and no surplus for household and

And God is able to make all grace abound to you, so that in all things at all times, having all that you need, you will abound in every good work.
— 2 Corinthians 9:8

living expenses, Janet's salary was her family's only income. Her job was critical.

Soon Janet learned that her situation had nothing to do with her performance. The fact that she was an excellent educator didn't matter in the  face of the school district's financial situation. With no warning, over thirty teachers received layoff notices, and she was one of them.

During the next two months, Janet watched as most of her fellow teachers salvaged their jobs; others left the area or retired. Only a handful, Janet included, were left without a job.

One night near the end of the summer break Janet prayed for the Shepherd's provision. "I'm a teacher without a job, and my family needs what I earn. What do you have in mind?"

The Shepherd's words, "I have something better in mind," were all that Janet needed to hear.

Somehow, despite her disappointment and worry, she knew things would be fine. Janet's one-way, thirty-mile commute across their mountain valley had taken time away from her family and was sometimes treacherous during snow season. Now Janet had a strong impression that God was going to get her a job closer to home.

With a month left until the first day of school, others encouraged Janet to apply for available jobs, but those positions were even farther from home. Janet continued to trust that the Shepherd had something better in mind.

One week before school started in their little town, Janet got a call from the local high-school principal. Two of his English teachers had just given retirement notices and he needed someone to do a long-term substitute job. He also encouraged Janet to apply for a permanent position. The something better in mind was a job just ninety seconds away from their home in the same school where her two older kids would attend. She also received a significant increase in pay and had fewer expenses because of working close to home.

Had Janet not been laid off, she would never have been able to work minutes from home for an increased salary. As an added bonus, Janet has had three of her four children in her class. "The Lord had something better in mind for me," she says. "And I've learned that hard times always have a greater purpose."

Being laid off can be heartbreaking no matter the reason. For Renee it wasn't downsizing that caused her financial situation to change. Even before her husband, Dave, was diagnosed with a long-term neurological illness, he had begun a steady decline that caused him to lose a high-paying job as a national sales manager for a television station. He struggled to sell insurance and home alarm systems but was successful at neither.

Trust the past to God's mercy, the present to God's love and the future to God's providence.
—St. Augustine

Renee became the primary breadwinner for her family that included two sons ages twelve and nine. A few short months after Dave lost his job, Renee was offered a position with a large national corporation that not only doubled her salary but also had an attractive year-end performance incentive. She thanked the Shepherd for providing the increase in her earning potential, even though it was not enough to recoup the large salary Dave had been earning in his successful television career.

Renee continued to rob money from savings to make their house payment each month, and their growing credit-card debt caused more than one sleepless night. "Why me?" Renee cried many times that year. She knew the Shepherd promised to provide, but she still felt overwhelmed by the mounting debt.

After her first year at the new job, Renee's prayers to the Shepherd were answered in the form of an employment offer with a significant raise in earning potential. The only negative was  that she had not qualified for the year-end performance incentive. Still, she had earned a nice income and was thankful to God for the opportunities that had thrust her career into high gear almost as swiftly as Dave's profession had diminished. With the salary increase, Renee figured she could eventually chip away at the huge credit-card debt they had amassed.

Shortly after beginning her new job, Renee opened the mailbox one Saturday and found an envelope from her previous employer. Inside was a very large check. *This has to be a mistake.* Renee rubbed her eyes as she remembered that the company had already settled any vacation or personal days owed her at the time she left. *There's no way I can keep this money.*

"What's the deal with this check I just got?"

asked Renee when she called a former coworker.

"The sales goals were recalculated at the end of the year," he explained. "We all qualified for the year-end bonus."

After she hung up Renee held the check for a long time. Then she pulled out one credit-card statement after another and added the balances. The total came to a mere forty dollars of paying off a five-figure debt. Renee cried tears of joy and fell to her knees with a thankful prayer.

Renee's hard times have helped to build the faith she continues to need as her husband declines. "I think about that day often. I know it was a miracle," she says. "I almost feel like God was knocking on my head saying, 'Wake up, Renee, it's God. I'm here for you. You don't have to do this all by yourself.'"

Two women—one from losing a job, the other through a disability—learned that the Shepherd will always provide. Not always according to our schedule nor always how we expect, but he always has something better in mind.

Before they call I will answer;
while they are still speaking I will hear.
—Isaiah 65:24

He who waits on God never waits too long.
—Chuck Wagner

NOW THANK WE ALL OUR GOD

MARTIN RINKART

Now we thank we all our God, with heart and hands and voices,

Who wondrous things has done, in Whom this world rejoices;

Who from our mothers' arms has blessed us on our way

With countless gifts of love, and still is ours today.

O may this bounteous God through all our life be near us,

With ever joyful hearts and blessed peace to cheer us;

And keep us in His grace, and guide us when perplexed;

And free us from all ills, in this world and the next!

CHAPTER THREE

THE SHEPHERD OF

Rest

"HE MAKES ME LIE DOWN IN GREEN PASTURES"

A THUMBTACK MIRACLE

"I just want to welcome you," said Diane's neighbor as she stood before the rental house.

"Thank you," mumbled Diane, a pregnant mother of four. "Nice to meet you, too." She turned to walk back to her new home.

Any other time Diane would have rejoiced that she had friendly neighbors, but now all she could dwell on were her losses. Just a week ago, Diane was cooking when she realized she didn't have everything for a class she was teaching at church that night. Knowing a quick trip would take only a few minutes, she turned down the heat under the skillet, jumped into the car, and drove to the store.

My soul is weary with sorrow; strengthen me according to your word.
—Psalm 119:28

- 19 -

Diane saw her house in flames less than fifteen minutes later as she rounded the corner and drove up their street.

"My babies! Where are my babies?" Diane's first thought was for her four children, ages twelve, ten, three, and one. Once she knew her children were out of the house and safe, the reality of the fire set in. A group of neighbors huddled on the lawn watching her house and all the family's belongings burning.

This can't be happening. How will I tell Vince I burned down the house? Where will we live? Diane stood in the bitter cold January that evening at dusk wondering how to contact her husband, Vince, a long-distance truck driver who was now two thousand miles away in California.

Eventually, the firemen finished their job, and the Red Cross located a room for Diane and her children to sleep in for a few nights until she could find a house to rent. Knowing she had to be strong for her children, she held her emotions together until Vince got home on Saturday.

Guilty thoughts plagued Diane as she played the what-if game during the day. Each night she'd worry herself to sleep only to awaken and find that nothing had changed. She worked with various agencies to get clothing and personal items for the children and herself and did her best to put on a brave face. When Vince finally arrived home, Diane flew into his arms. The tears she had tried to quell finally broke like the waters of the Mississippi during a spring rain.

Diane and Vince left the children with her parents and drove back to the house, wondering if anything could be salvaged. Sitting on what was left of their front porch in the freezing cold after an ice storm, Diane felt her heart break into tiny pieces with each discovered loss.

"The Christmas ornaments! Those are irreplaceable," she reminded Vince. Even though it made her feel worse, she couldn't help remembering unique decorations made by her children or given by someone special. "Everything's gone. How will we ever survive?"

Exhausted and morning sick, Diane began the process of starting over. She and Vince sifted through the rubble, filled out more insurance forms than they thought possible, and found a rental house.

A week after the fire, Vince was back on the road, and Diane and her four children, the two smallest with pneumonia thanks to a combination of smoke inhalation and freezing temperatures, moved into their new home. Walking inside, Diane's depression nearly overwhelmed her. Boxes of donated linens sat in the empty rooms.

"What are we going to sleep on?" asked ten-year-old Mark. "There're no beds."

I will find rest nowhere but in His holy will, a will that is unspeakably beyond my largest notions of what He is up to.
—Elisabeth Elliot

"No table or chairs either," piped up his older brother, Troy. "I want to go home."

Diane looked around trying to find something good about the empty house. Then she saw them. "Boys, look at these great windows. Every room will be filled with light and we can look out and see what's happening."

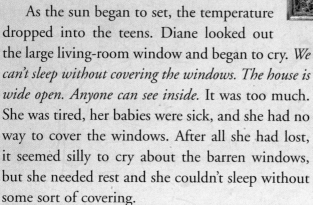

As the sun began to set, the temperature dropped into the teens. Diane looked out the large living-room window and began to cry. *We can't sleep without covering the windows. The house is wide open. Anyone can see inside.* It was too much. She was tired, her babies were sick, and she had no way to cover the windows. After all she had lost, it seemed silly to cry about the barren windows, but she needed rest and she couldn't sleep without some sort of covering.

Diane sorted through a box of linens hoping to find curtains. Instead, all she found were sheets for whenever they got beds. *If I had nails, I could cover those windows,* thought Diane. She looked through their few possessions, but there was nothing that would work. Because of the pneumonia, and her sick children, she couldn't leave them alone and go to a store.

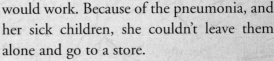

"*Lord, please help me figure something out,*" Diane prayed. And then the doorbell rang. Diane walked to the door, opened it, and there stood her brother, Harvey.

"Hey, Diane," he said as he walked inside. "I found something your boys might enjoy."

He handed Mark a box of baseball cards he had found in the attic of his recently purchased home. Forgetting the lack of furniture and curtains. Mark dumped the cards to the floor.

"I don't believe it!" screamed Diane. "No way!"

There, in the jumble of cards, lay dozens of thumbtacks. With more shouts of joy, Diane scooped up the tacks, pulled out the sheets, and ran to the first window. The Shepherd had answered her prayer. She and Harvey covered each window with the sheets. There were exactly enough thumb-tacks, not one too few or too many.

Diane rested the first night in her new home secure that if the Shepherd provided tacks to a worn-out, brokenhearted woman he would surely take care of all the other details from the fire. Better still, she knew that no matter what the future held, the Shepherd would always grant rest to her weary soul.

Do not be anxious about anything, but in everything, by prayer and petition, with thanksgiving, present your requests to God.
—Philippians 4:6

Nothing is too great and nothing is too small to commit into the hands of the Lord.
—A. W. Pink

I HEARD THE VOICE OF JESUS SAY

HORATIUS BONAR

I heard the voice of Jesus say, "Come unto Me and rest;

Lay down, thou weary one, lay down Thy head upon My breast."

I came to Jesus as I was, Weary and worn and sad;

I found in Him a resting-place, and He has made me glad.

CHAPTER FOUR

THE SHEPHERD OF *Peace*

"HE LEADS ME BESIDE QUIET WATERS"

PEACEFUL WORDS

I can't let you go until I know you've heard me say good-bye, thought Anne as she watched her mother. The elderly woman had lived a good, full life, but Anne wasn't ready to say good-bye. Miriam had been unresponsive for days. She occasionally smiled when she heard a familiar voice, but more often than not, Miriam lay silent, not stirring as much as a muscle.

Thanks to the kindness of the nurses, Anne was allowed great flexibility in visiting hours. They knew that she kept vigil in the waiting room down the hall from the neurological intensive-care unit, and they would get her if things were running

LORD, you establish peace for us; all that we have accomplished you have done for us.
—Isaiah 26:12

smoothly with the other patients. "Sit with her, if you want," they told Anne. "Her vital signs are better when you're here."

Anne either sat beside her mother's bed or stood quietly in the corner of her cubicle, keeping watch.

Sometimes Anne held her hand or stroked her arm, grieving her nonresponsiveness. She longed for serenity, but watching her beloved mother drift away splintered her heart. A multitude of emotions played havoc with the outward calm she desperately needed. How could she be sure her mother knew she was there? Remembering that some of Miriam's favorite Scripture verses were in Psalm 23, Anne decided to try something.

"I'm going to say some Bible verses for you," Anne said, taking her mother's hand in hers and lightly stroking it. "Let me know if I mess up."

"The Lord is my Shepherd" she began to recite. She continued, deliberately leaving out a couple of words. Immediately, Miriam squeezed her daughter's fingers. "Oops," Anne said, excited with the response. "Let me try again."

This time Anne said the verse correctly and was rewarded by the tiniest hint of a smile. Brushing away tears, Anne started on the next verse. She stumbled over the words, and once again came the slight pressure on her hand. Anne leaned down to kiss Miriam's forehead. "You do hear me, don't you?" she whispered. A barely perceptible nod of Miriam's head made Anne grin as she caught the lingering smile on her mother's face.

"He leads me beside quiet waters," said Anne as an unexplainable peace filled the room. Miriam's condition had not changed, yet with each line Anne's anxiety diminished.

Anne spent the next hour or so quietly murmuring verses to Miriam, rejoicing each time her mother pressed her hand when she intentionally made a mistake. Miriam's fingers, the strong fin-

First keep the peace within yourself, then you can also bring peace to others.
—Thomas à Kempis

gers of a lifelong pianist, were now weak and chilly, but each time they squeezed a signal, Anne felt as if she'd received a wonderful gift.

Those precious moments were the last that Miriam was able to communicate with Anne. As  the Shepherd led the older woman through the valley of the shadow of death, a lifetime of walking with the Lord made the difference to both women. Anne's voice, combined with words powerful enough to reach through a coma-induced fog, brought peace to a brokenhearted daughter and prepared a mother for an eternity with the Shepherd.

Those who walk uprightly enter into peace;
they find rest as they lie in death.
—Isaiah 57:1, 2

Peace is our gift to each other.
—Elie Wiesel

THE LORD BLESS YOU AND KEEP YOU

PETER C. LUTKIN

The Lord bless you and keep you.

The Lord lift His countenance upon you,

And give you peace, and give you peace.

The Lord make His face to shine upon you,

And be gracious, and be gracious;

The Lord be gracious, gracious unto you.

CHAPTER FIVE

THE SHEPHERD OF

Hope

"HE RESTORES MY SOUL"

DAVID'S GOOFY DAY

Several years ago, actor Michael J. Fox was diagnosed with Parkinson's disease. I wondered how someone so nice could have such a horrible fate. This wasn't some misbehaving, Hollywood bad boy. This was Alex P. Keaton, the likable Republican, economics-loving, wisecracking kid on *Family Ties*. How could Alex P. Keaton have Parkinson's? I've never met Michael J. Fox and probably never will, but I hurt for him and his family. They must have been brokenhearted to learn the news.

Because our family had already been dealing with another neurological disorder for several years, I could relate to the Fox family. Of course,

Therefore my heart is glad and my tongue rejoices; my body also will live in hope.
—Acts 2:26

because it was my husband, my finances, and my life, I felt that our burdens were much greater than anything in the universe.

In an interview on Larry King Live, Michael J. Fox made a profound statement: "When something enters your life that is so big and so non-negotiable as catastrophic illness, you either go in denial for a while, or ultimately you accept it, and you make space for it.... You simply look at the world differently."

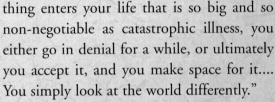

Huntington's disease is one of those non-negotiables. You are born with the gene even though symptoms might not creep up until you are middle-aged. It affects both the mind and the body, and has no cure. Unlike Parkinson's, which has millions of sufferers and major research dollars, Huntington's is what they call an orphan disease. So few people are affected that it almost doesn't matter, except to families who hope and pray for a cure. Similar to Michael J. Fox, brokenhearted people have to look at the world differently and to find hope in unconventional ways.

A few years ago, I looked at my husband differently than I ever thought I would. At forty-six years of age, David shuffled through his days like an old man of eighty. As his appetite and ability to swallow continued to decrease, so did his weight. Sometimes I wasn't sure who lived in his body: a three-year-old child or an old man who sat and stared into space.

During one period of about two years, my husband was obsessed with Goofy. It might be common for those with Huntington's to be obsessive compulsive, but it's enough to drive others mad to be around them during this phase. For Christmas I gave him his heart's desire —two Goofy shirts that he wore almost exclusively. It came as no surprise that David wanted to go to Disney World to see his hero.

I could never have afforded Disney tickets for

my family of four, but I wanted to give David a special day. Thanks to the generosity of the wonderful Disney Compassion Program, David, dressed in his purple Goofy shirt, got his wish and we set off for the Magic Kingdom.

As excited as David was about the excursion, I had a nagging concern. What if we got to the park and couldn't find Goofy? It might sound odd, but before we left I prayed that we'd find Goofy. The rest of the day could be hot with long lines, but we had to find Goofy.

Right inside the front gate, holding court to dozens of young fans clutching their autograph books, faces glowing as they excitedly waited to greet him, was the answer to our prayers. I wheeled David's chair up the ramp and stood behind the children, none of them older than five. I alternated between feeling happy for David, embarrassed because of his age and disability, and brokenhearted at the loss of my dreams. At that moment, I had to look at David

Most of the important things in the world have been accomplished by people who have kept on trying when there seemed to be no hope at all.
—Dale Carnegie

and myself differently. Before Huntington's disease ravaged his brain, David had earned a masters of business administration degree. He was himself a parent, yet now the crowning achievement in his life was to spend time with Goofy.

Finally, it was David's turn. His face was one ecstatic smile, and Goofy seemed to know he was special. Instead of the brief time spent with the kids, Goofy gave David a hug, a caress on the arm with the floppy ear, a kiss on the cheek, posing for pictures, and another hug. Because our photos needed developing, a lady with a Polaroid camera took a picture for David to carry around all day. I tried hard to smile, but it was difficult to breathe as I watched David's childlike delight through a veil of tears.

We bought a turquoise Goofy shirt and a colorful doll. Every few minutes David pulled Goofy out of the bag and talked to him. Since his wheelchair got the royal treatment, we didn't have to cope with lines as we breezed through the park. David and Goofy enjoyed every ride, even the scary ones. That night he slept with Goofy and woke me up to find the doll whenever it got tangled in the covers or fell to the floor.

Norman Vincent Peale said, "Hope is wanting something so eagerly that—in spite of all the evidence that you're not going to get it—you go right on wanting it." For the ten years David lived with Huntington's disease I never stopped hoping. At first my hopes led me to pray for a cure, even though the evidence was against that happening in David's lifetime. As the Shepherd began to heal my heart, I realized that our hopes lay not in an earthly cure but in the Shepherd's eternal salvation. For David, Huntington's stripped him of everything except infinity with the Shepherd.

Of all my memories, David's Goofy day breaks

my heart the most yet still makes me smile. Part of me was happy to give David his Goofy day, and the other half was in mourning for the husband I had already said good-bye to years before.

In his CNN interview, Michael J. Fox described Parkinson's as "a gift that keeps on taking. But it's certainly a gift." Before persons can see the Shepherd face-to-face, they have to experience loss. Huntington's took David's mind and body, but he never lost his faith. Today David is enjoying the Shepherd's sacrificial gift of eternal salvation.

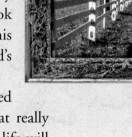

Living with Huntington's strengthened my faith and taught me to hope for what really matters. Other things that happen in my life will break my heart, but my hope in the Shepherd's promise will always heal me.

*May the God of hope fill you with all joy and peace
as you trust in him, so that you may overflow with
hope by the power of the Holy Spirit.*
—Romans 15:13

*Hope begins in the dark, the stubborn hope
that if you just show up and try to do the
right thing, the dawn will come.*
—Anne Lamott

THE SOLID ROCK

Edward Mote

His oath, His covenant, His blood,

Support me in the whelming flood.

When all around my soul gives way,

He then is all my Hope and Stay.

On Christ, the solid Rock, I stand,

All other ground is sinking sand.

All other ground is sinking sand.

CHAPTER SIX

THE
SHEPHERD WHO
Directs

"HE GUIDES ME IN PATHS OF RIGHTEOUSNESS FOR HIS NAME'S SAKE"

MUSTARD-SEED FAITH

After an abusive first marriage, Carol, a single mother with three teenaged daughters, thought she would be alone for the rest of her life. Her heart had a chance to heal, and then the Michigan native met and married again. When her twin sons were ten years old, their father suffered a heart attack.

Something isn't right. We'll never make it there in time. Why don't they go faster?

Carol's unspoken questions as she rode in the ambulance were answered when they arrived at the hospital. "I'm so sorry," said the emergency-room physician. "He died before they ever left your driveway."

Whether you turn to the right or to the left, your ears will hear a voice behind you, saying, "This is the way; walk in it."

—Isaiah 30:21

As much as Carol wanted to nurse her shattered heart, she had her children to think about. Her brother had moved to Florida and Carol followed, deciding a change of location would help everyone.

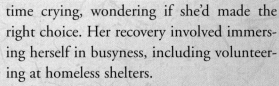

She missed her friends and spent much of her time crying, wondering if she'd made the right choice. Her recovery involved immersing herself in busyness, including volunteering at homeless shelters.

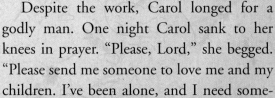

Despite the work, Carol longed for a godly man. One night Carol sank to her knees in prayer. "Please, Lord," she begged. "Please send me someone to love me and my children. I've been alone, and I need someone to love and take care of us." After she prayed, she experienced a sense of peace and fell asleep.

Soon after her plea, Carol met John, and they were married a year later. Carol continued her volunteer work with the homeless, always elated when she located affordable apartments for families in transition. But she soon discovered a painful reality. "I've brought these people to their new homes," she told John, "and now I realize they have absolutely nothing to put in them. They have no beds for the kids. They all huddle on the floor with just an old jacket spread over them. I can't walk away from that."

So it was that, directed by the Shepherd, out of her own pocket and with neighbors and churches donating furniture and other needed items, she helped set up a household for a single mother with three little boys.

Helping the homeless and those who had lost everything due to catastrophic situations filled Carol with an excitement unlike any other she had experienced. John had a well paying job, and Carol continued to work part-time, but still money trickled out of their bank account as they frequented neighborhood stores to buy necessities for a growing number of families.

As the number of needy families increased, Carol prayed, and the Shepherd answered, "Start your own program."

Carol knew what it was like to lose everything, and those memories fueled her passion. Armed  with that passion and the knowledge that God knew what He was doing even if she didn't, Carol got into her car one day. "It was as if my hands were on the steering wheel, but I wasn't driving," she says. "I turned right and about a half-a-mile away, I saw a blue sign that said, 'Warehouses for Rent.'" She told her story to the warehouse manager who gave her a discount, and she signed the paperwork.

Heading back on the main road, she turned left and pulled into a U-Haul location. Again she explained her business and told them of her goal to help the homeless. The manager called their corporate office, and they arranged for a discount. Next, the local paper refused payment for an ad soliciting furniture and other household items.

The paraphrased Scripture verse, "If you have faith the size of a mustard seed, you can move mountains," became Carol's foundation for the organization. That year, with the help of many who gave possessions they no longer needed, Carol and John furnished homes for ninety-nine families.

Then disaster hit. Just as the Mustard Seed ministry was growing, John's company downsized, and he lost his job. "We have a situation here," John said. "This would be a good time for you to work full time while I job hunt. There's no way I can pay all these bills by myself."

"But John," Carol cried. "It just breaks my heart to see people who have lost everything. If we don't help them, who will?"

"The only way we can keep the Mustard Seed open is to sell the house. Is that what you really want?"

Life is short and we never have enough time for gladdening the hearts of those who travel the way with us.
—Henri Frederic Amiel

Carol was totally at peace with selling all they had to continue helping others. Her remarkable husband agreed. With only enough money left for one house payment, Carol asked God to arrange for a quick sale of their home or to find a job for John. With twenty-five days to vacate, the house sold.

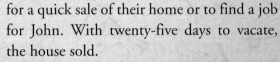

When Carol realized how much she'd given up, she felt torn apart inside. She wept harder that night than she ever had before. Cried out and exhausted, the Lord moved Carol and John to a rental house and later into an even smaller apartment. But the Mustard Seed continued to flourish.

Eventually, John found a job. Armed with their remaining funds and needing to buy a house or pay a significant capital-gains tax, John and Carol began their search.

On one of their house-hunting forays, the Christian Realtor and Carol stopped in front of a two story house that was reminiscent of Michigan architecture. Owned by a builder, the house had never been lived in. As if waiting for them, it had stood empty the entire time John was unemployed. They placed an offer on the house, and though much lower than the asking price, the owner accepted it. Obtaining a no-money-down Veteran's Administration mortgage, and with remaining funds, they were able to replace their own furniture they had given to needy families.

From a broken heart, the Shepherd grew in Carol a hunger to help broken people rebuild their lives. Following the Shepherd's direction, since 1986 Carol and The Mustard Seed Furniture Bank, now a United Way charity, have helped over thirty-two thousand families receive complete households of furniture and other items. Thousands more each year receive clothing, food, and holiday meals and gifts.

People wonder how Carol could give up her house and furniture for strangers. But she says, "I've seen how little it takes to heal broken hearts. How could I not? I love the *people* part of running the organization. Certain people come in who need love. That's what I'm the best at."

Teach me to do your will, for you are my God; may your good spirit lead me on level ground.

——Psalm 143:10

Each of us may be sure that if God sends us on stony paths He will provide us with strong shoes, and He will not send us out on any journey for which He does not equip us well.

——Alexander MacLaren

TRUST AND OBEY

John H. Sammis

Not a burden we bear, Not a sorrow we share,

But our toil He doth richly repay.

Not a grief nor a loss, Not a frown nor a cross

But is blest if we trust and obey.

CHAPTER SEVEN

THE SHEPHERD OF *Patience*

"EVEN THOUGH I WALK THROUGH THE VALLEY OF THE SHADOW OF DEATH"

PREPARED FOR SOMETHING

After a night of bowling, Charles slowed the car to make a right turn at the traffic light and noticed a man waiting to cross the street. Just before braking, Charles observed the man's hesitation, took the lead, and began a slow turn.

Suddenly, the man ran up to the driver's side and began tapping on the window with a gun. With shaking hands, Charles opened the passenger-side door and the man got inside.

"Drive!" yelled the carjacker.

"Take the car. Just don't shoot me," pleaded the

Be joyful in hope, patient in affliction, faithful in prayer.
—Romans 12:12

married father of two. He drove until forced to stop at a secluded area.

"Give me the keys."

Please, Lord, get me out of this alive. Just as Charles reached out to hand over the keys, the assailant took aim and fired. Charles dropped the keys. The man took his eyes off his victim long enough to find and scoop up the keys. Almost without thinking, Charles used his distraction to open the door, fall from the car, and make a run for it. An excruciating stab shot the length of his leg as he tried to run and then collapsed. He later learned the fall completed the break begun when a bullet from the .38 caliber handgun shattered his thigh.

Gasping in pain, Charles crept behind some nearby shrubs to hide. When he heard the man drive away, Charles crawled to the nearest house. "Help me!" he cried. "I've been shot."

The door remained closed, and Charles, too exhausted to move, lay still, wondering if this was how his life would end. A few minutes later, he heard a police siren. The woman in the house had telephoned the police who called for an ambulance.

Several miles away, the incessant ringing of the phone at 6:00 a.m. roused Cynthia from a deep sleep.

"Do you realize that your husband is a patient here?"

"A patient? Who is this?" responded Cynthia, totally confused.

"We've been calling all night," said the voice from the hospital.

"Oh, I guess I never heard the phone. Who is this?"

Cynthia learned that Charles had been shot and that the doctors were having trouble stabilizing his blood pressure. Hanging up, she dressed, called her work to let them know she wouldn't be in, and asked a neighbor to come and stay with her four-year-old son and one-year-old daughter.

"Please be patient," the nurses told Cynthia when she arrived at the emergency room. She

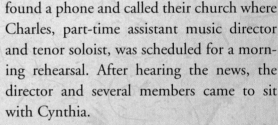

found a phone and called their church where Charles, part-time assistant music director and tenor soloist, was scheduled for a morning rehearsal. After hearing the news, the director and several members came to sit with Cynthia.

"Just a little while longer," became the nurses' stock answer as Cynthia's vigil continued. *I just have to be patient*, thought Cynthia as she prayed to the Shepherd. She had no idea how many years she would have to be patient.

Eight hours later, the doctor explained that Charles had lost a great deal of blood and received several units. "Because of the placement, we left the bullet in for now. We've repaired his leg with a metal rod."

Charles and Cynthia never doubted that the Shepherd was in control of their situation. Because of a switch from their traditional insurance provider to an HMO just months before the incident, every medical expense was covered. Family, friends, and church members rallied around the family, providing meals, money, visits, transportation to therapy, and help around the house.

Three months of physical therapy helped Charles graduate from two crutches to one, and eventually to a cane. He resumed his full-time job as a juvenile court probation officer and his part-time position at the church. A lifelong blood donor, he even felt well enough to donate blood. In 1985, nearly one year after the shooting, both the bullet and the metal rod came out of his leg. Life was back to normal . . . they thought.

Then, shortly after his last surgery, Charles took his son to Florida to visit relatives. While he was gone, Cynthia signed for a certified letter for him from the American Red Cross. Shocked, she discovered that her husband's blood was found to contain the HIV virus. Cynthia called the contact person only to learn that Charles was indeed the intended recipient of the letter. Charles returned home to find a brokenhearted wife. They cried and hugged and prayed . . . and waited.

As the couple waited for the proverbial shoe to drop, the stress took a toll on their marriage. Charles was concerned about the stigma of AIDS and what it would do to their family. The once intimate pair now lived as roommates, a silent partnership-in-waiting for some kind of HIV-related symptom that didn't come. The sense of humor and gentle teasing that first drew Cynthia to Charles were all but gone.

"I hate being called Cindy," remembers Cynthia.

The keys to patience are acceptance and faith. Accept things as they are, and look realistically at the world around you.
—Ralph Marston

"As our marriage grew more strained I'd have given anything to hear him try to get a rise by calling me by that detested name." Instead, the walls of silence—coupled with work, parenting, and worry—brought her to a point where there were no feelings left.

In 1989, four years after learning about HIV, Cynthia had enough. "I had no choice but to be patient and continue waiting for symptoms, but it didn't mean I had to wait in the same house with a man I no longer loved." Cynthia found an apartment, but before she signed the lease, she prayed one last time.

Charles' response when she told him about the apartment was, "How can I save my family?" That was enough to convince her that the Shepherd had a different plan. A close friend noticed the strain and suggested counseling, and, over time, the Shepherd brought healing and renewed love to their marriage.

In November 2003, more than nineteen years

after the transfusions, Charles began losing weight. His appetite tapered off, and he developed a nagging cold. Cynthia's carefully constructed wall of protection around her heart began to crumble as she realized what the symptoms meant. In January Charles finally went to see the doctor. By February, after a week in the hospital, the wait was over. The tests were positive.

"I cried and cried," says Cynthia. "I knew he could get AIDS, but after so long we had both hoped that the letter had been sent to the wrong person." Over the years, they had avoided talking about what they would do if the inevitable happened. Now they had no choice but to trust the Shepherd. Charles' fear that people would retreat once they learned the news never materialized. Instead, family, friends, pastors, and musicians from around the country showed their support through letters, calls, and visits.

In April doctors diagnosed a severe headache as

viral meningitis. Two weeks later Charles underwent a new series of tests because of his slurred speech and confusion. The CAT scan showed a lesion on his brain symptomatic of the HIV virus. He now had full-blown AIDS. "The day we got the news, May 30, was especially hard. It was my birthday and he didn't even know it," Cynthia says.

Charles spent June 5, their twenty-eighth anniversary, deathly ill from the strong antibiotics. By June 7 the doctors suggested that Cynthia call anyone wanting to spend quality time with Charles to come as quickly as possible. From around the country, people came, and throughout the world they prayed. Instead of getting worse as the doctor predicted, however, Charles began to improve.

A few months later the doctor shared a prediction with Cynthia that was like healing balm to her hurting heart.

"Your husband needs to get himself ready to play with his grandchildren," he said with a smile.

Because neither of their children were married nor engaged, this was the doctor's way of saying that their patience and prayers had paid off for a long life.

Reflecting on her growth during this time, Cynthia remembers that she couldn't stop reading her Bible during the Christmas of 1983. "I read and read and read as if my body needed that kind of food, or I would die," she explains. "I felt like I was reading because I was being prepared for something, but I wasn't sure what. Now I know."

I waited patiently for the L<small>ORD</small>;
he turned to me and heard my cry.
—Psalm 40:1

A man without patience is a lamp without oil.
—Andres Segovia

HOW FIRM A FOUNDATION

JOHN RIPPON'S SELECTION OF HYMNS

Fear not; I am with thee, Oh, be not dismayed,

For I am thy God, I will still give thee aid.

I'll strengthen thee, help thee, and cause thee to stand,

Upheld by My gracious, omnipotent hand.

CHAPTER EIGHT

THE
SHEPHERD OF

Courage

"I WILL FEAR NO EVIL"

THE COURAGE TO FORGIVE

The year Melanie turned eight, her mother was diagnosed with multiple sclerosis. A year later, Melanie's father, Curtis, started sneaking into her bedroom at night. The two cataclysmic events in the young girl's life may have been related, but at the time, all Melanie knew was that she no longer had a safe harbor.

By the time Melanie turned fifteen she was actively fighting off her father and spending more time on the streets. Even the drug houses that populated the area were more appealing than home.

Shortly after Melanie turned sixteen, she approached her father with dread. "I'm pregnant,

Have I not commanded you? Be strong and courageous. Do not be terrified; do not be discouraged, for the LORD your God will be with you wherever you go.

—Joshua 1:9

Dad," she confessed knowing instinctively what his reaction would be.

Feeling she had no other option, Melanie agreed to his demand that she have an abortion. Years later, she wondered whose child she had aborted.

Like many sexually abused children, Melanie's shame and guilt kept her from telling anyone about her father. Maybe they would blame her, tell her she had asked for it. Besides, her confession would affect her mother who was ill much of the time. Melanie's love for her mother ensured her silence as well as her care. When she was seventeen, however, her mother died, and Melanie was heartbroken.

Once away from home, Melanie finished school, worked, and met Michael, whom she later married. On the surface, things were fine, but Melanie considered herself a murderer, and she shouldered the blame for her shattered past. When she became pregnant again, Melanie knew she had to change her life for her child's sake.

Melanie's maternal grandparents lived quite a distance away, but growing up she envied their lifestyle of peace and happiness. Their orderly and loving home was a house inhabited by God, and they lived out their faith in count-  less ways. She remained silent about her home life in the beginning because of her father's threats to stop her summer visits. In the end, she didn't want her beloved grandparents to know what their granddaughter had become.

With the upcoming birth of her daugh- ter, Melanie set out to discover their God, and they eagerly instructed her. Through the Bible, Melanie learned that she had a heavenly Father who would never abuse or leave her. She also learned that the Shepherd forgives sin—all sin. Nothing was unforgivable in his eyes.

Sure, God can forgive, but I can never forgive Dad

for what he did, thought the young woman who had been wronged in the worst possible way. *My father did something to me that twisted years of my life.* Still, the lure of a heavenly Father and forgiveness set Melanie on a faith journey.

Despite her growing love for the Shepherd, she could not quite let go of what could have been. Of all the commandments, one became imprinted on her heart: "Honor your father and mother." But how do you honor someone who has done something so dishonorable?

In Matthew 6: 15 Melanie read, "If you do not forgive men their sins, your Father will not forgive your sins." What her father had done was heinous, but, with the Shepherd's help, it wasn't unforgivable. She realized that her unwillingness to forgive him was a sin and the only way to patch together the pieces of her broken heart was for her to forgive her father and accept the Shepherd's forgiveness. As she continued to pray, Melanie

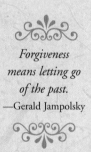

Forgiveness means letting go of the past.
—Gerald Jampolsky

yearned even more to see him become a part of God's family. That thought gave Melanie the courage to forge a relationship with her father.

The courage to get to know and subsequently forgive her dad did not come easily. Mark Twain said, "Courage is not the lack of fear. It is acting in spite of it." Melanie feared rejection from her father, but, with the Shepherd's prodding, she began to love and eventually forgive him.

In the last three years of his life, emphysema, combined with a heart that was five times its normal size, left Melanie's father almost helpless. Honoring him became more than a line in a list of dos and don'ts as Melanie cared for him every day during those three years. They talked about many things but never the abuse. He did, however, talk about his childhood. Learning how his parents treated him, particularly his father, explained how deprived his life had been. It didn't justify his actions, but it did somehow make it easier for Melanie to continue the forgiveness process.

Melanie talked to her father about her growing relationship with the Shepherd and how He also loved him and would welcome him with open arms. Her father, Curtis, listened but commented very little.

One month before his death, Melanie dropped in to pick up his laundry and bring him food. Inside she found him crying at the dining-room table.

Thinking his health had worsened, Melanie asked, "What's wrong, Dad?"

Bracing herself for the worst, Melanie heard the words she never dreamed her dad would utter. "I treated you so awful! I'm so sorry!"

Melanie stood in the doorway, speechless. Then, for the first time in her memory, she enveloped her father in a heartfelt hug, whispering, "I forgive you."

According to Melanie's aunt, Melanie and her

dad spent hours on the phone talking about God and forgiveness, and she believes that he accepted Christ in the end. Malachi 4:6 says, "He will turn the hearts of the fathers to their children, and the hearts of the children to their fathers." Thanks to the Shepherd, father and daughter found the courage to turn their hearts to each other.

Now Melanie says, "I am grateful to God that He gave me the strength and faith to complete my relationship with my father. If my aunt is correct, I will see him on the other side of the veil."

And when you stand praying, if you hold anything against anyone, forgive him, so that your Father in heaven may forgive you your sins.

——Mark 11:25

Forgiveness is the answer to the child's dream of a miracle by which what is broken is made whole again, what is soiled is again made clean.
—Dag Hammarskjold

GRACE GREATER THAN OUR SIN

JULIA H. JOHNSTON

Marvelous grace of our loving Lord,

Grace that exceeds our sin and our guilt,

Yonder on Calvary's mount outpoured,

There where the blood of the Lamb was spilt!

CHAPTER NINE

THE
SHEPHERD OF

Friends

"FOR YOU ARE WITH ME"

FRIEND IN NEED, FRIEND IN DEED

My loneliness dissolved when I met Kathy on the first day at my new school. She was pretty and dressed with the understated confidence of someone accustomed to having money. I, on the other hand, made do with much less, but the disparity in our backgrounds never made a difference. Kathy and I had many common interests; we even sang in the school choir together. We giggled and talked as if we had known each other for years. Kathy's popularity helped open doors that might have remained firmly shut to me in the adolescent world of cliques. Soon, I felt as if I'd always attended this junior high.

A man of many companions may come to ruin, but there is a friend who sticks closer than a brother.
—Proverbs 18:24

One day Kathy announced she was having a slumber birthday party. My being invited to this party by such a popular girl was exciting and signaled acceptance. Besides the snacks, I needed a sleeping bag, a pillow, and a multitude of other teenage "must-haves." I can still see the pristine white-cotton lace ruffle around the neck of my most beautiful pajamas ever: brand-new, petal-pink baby dolls.

Finally, the momentous Friday evening arrived. I chattered nonstop as Mom drove me the few blocks to Kathy's house. I bounced out of the old car and scrambled up the long walkway to ring the bell, then waited impatiently, clutching my worn, shiny-blue sleeping bag to my chest.

When Kathy's mom opened the door, the smile on her lips did not reach her eyes. With a quizzical coolness, she glanced at my bright, shining face.

"Kathy can't come out this evening. She and her friends are having a birthday sleepover."

"I know about the party," I interrupted. "Kathy invited me." I held out the wrapped present as evidence, an admission ticket of sorts.

A sickening silence descended as the pinched smile faded from her lips. In its place was a cold, questioning look. She insisted I could come tomorrow but not tonight. Had I imagined the friendship and the invitation? A queasy stomach followed my unstoppable tears.

"Mom, hurry up," Kathy impatiently called as her mother delayed. Before her mother answered, Kathy rounded the corner and stood in the doorway. She had only to look at my tearful expression to see we had a problem.

"Mom, what's wrong?" she questioned. Her exasperated sigh and the gripping of her fists told me this was not the first time she had a run-in with her mother.

"Carmen is here to visit," her mother explained. "I told her to come back tomorrow because you're having a party."

Kathy's face turned crimson as she nervously glanced at me. "I invited Carmen to my party, Mom. She's my friend, and I want her here." I stood mortified as the discussion continued.

"This is a sleepover," replied her mother in hushed tones. "I can't have a colored girl sleep in our home."

A colored girl! Why did the color of my skin matter? Kathy was my best friend.

In an act of ultimate defiance and unparalleled friendship, Kathy firmly stood her ground. "Carmen is my friend. If she can't stay, no one stays. I won't have my party without her."

I couldn't believe that she was willing to cancel her birthday party on my behalf.

The only way to have a friend is to be one.
—Ralph Waldo Emerson

A look of consternation passed over her mother's face and hardened into a set mask. "All right. If that's want you want, go tell the girls."

Sometimes words are pointless. I choked with gratitude at this display of friendship. The girls quietly assembled under the cold, moonless sky to await their parents. I was suddenly nervous that the blame for the catastrophic end to the planned festivities would fall on my fragile shoulders. As Kathy and her mother argued inside the upper middle class home, I sat alone while the other girls spoke in whispers, glancing my way from time to time. As our parents arrived, we left the wide porch, burdened with our thoughts as well as our gear, and slipped quietly into the waiting cars.

On Monday, the reason for the aborted birthday party was the main topic of conversation at school. Most of my so-called friends looked through me as though I didn't exist.

Over the years when I've been heartbroken because of other's actions, I've thought about Kathy's selfless act. Long before someone coined the phrase, "What would Jesus do?" Kathy knew and lived the answer. I am sure that the Shepherd guided Kathy's decision to stand up for me. Her example of true friendship not only eased my heart that night, but it taught the value of a true friend.

My command is this: Love each
other as I have loved you.
—John 15:12

A friend is what the heart needs all the time.
—Henry Van Dyke

THE LILY OF THE VALLEY

CHARLES W. FRY

I've found a friend in Jesus, He's ev'rything to me.

He's the fairest of ten thousand to my soul.

The Lily of the Valley, in Him alone I see

All I need to cleanse and make me fully whole.

In sorrow He's my Comfort; in trouble He's my Stay.

He tells me ev'ry care on Him to roll.

He's the Lily of the Valley, the Bright and Morning Star.

He's the fairest of ten thousand to my soul.

CHAPTER TEN

THE SHEPHERD WHO

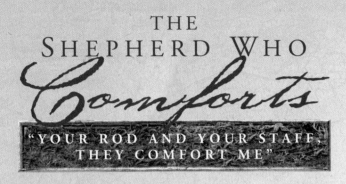

Comforts

"YOUR ROD AND YOUR STAFF, THEY COMFORT ME"

RING OF COMFORT

Laura couldn't believe the long-awaited day had finally come. As she sat in the chair, she admired how well the manicurist did her job. Laura didn't usually pamper herself, but today was a special day. She wanted to make sure her hands were a perfect complement to her rings.

Almost as if reading her mind, the woman held the pink-tipped brush in the air as she commented on Laura's ring. "Your engagement ring is beautiful."

"Thank you," said Linda with more than a touch of excitement. "Today I add the wedding

As a mother comforts her child, so will I comfort you.
—Isaiah 66:13

ring that matches it." Twisting the hand to admire both the ring and the newly polished nails, Laura thought about how in a few hours her hand would proclaim her status as a married woman.

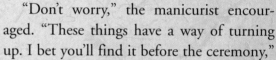

Then Laura's features clouded as she thought of the other ring. "I had an opal ring that I cherished," she told the woman, "but I foolishly lost it. I'd give anything to have it today as 'something old' for my wedding."

"Don't worry," the manicurist encouraged. "These things have a way of turning up. I bet you'll find it before the ceremony,"

Laura shook her head. "I don't think so. I've searched for that ring for years with no success. Anyway, what matters is today. In a few hours, I'll have a glittering wedding ring, and I'll never lose that one because it won't ever leave my finger."

The conversation turned to other topics, but on the way home to dress, Laura's thoughts returned to the lost ring. A gift from her mother, a single parent struggling to provide even the basics—let alone a special sweet sixteen gift, Laura had treasured the ring. Several years earlier while traveling, Laura had wrapped the ring in a tissue and tucked it into her suede purse for protection. Once home Laura frantically rummaged through the purse for the ring. No matter how often she looked, it wasn't there. After an hour of searching every square inch of the purse, including ripping apart the lining, Laura knew her treasured ring was gone.

Over time reminders of the ring would emerge, and she'd drag the purse out of the closet, searching all over again and praying, *Please, I'm begging you—make it appear.* Each time she went through the process, only to come up empty-handed, she vowed to throw the offending purse away. Laura even pitched it into the trash a few times, but within minutes, she always retrieved it.

One day the ring will miraculously appear. I know it will.

The wedding went as planned, and for a year-and-a-half, married life was wonderful. Then one day Laura's dream life came crashing down around her. That Saturday morning she was getting dressed to attend a women's luncheon with her mom and some friends. But she never made it to the event. The anticipated laughter of the day changed to crying, and the tears didn't stop for a long time.

"I want out, Laura," said Bruce entering their bedroom where she was getting ready.

"You want out? What does that mean?" Laura tried in vain to stop the tears from spilling over.

"Out."

Unable to speak, Laura looked with hindsight on the now-obvious clues. *Lord, show me what is wrong,* She prayed as she began to towel her hair dry. "Is there someone else?" she asked in a squeaky voice.

An ominous silence filled the room. Laura barely breathed as she waited for the answer.

"There could be," mumbled Bruce.

"There could be?" Laura snapped. "That's not an answer. I need a yes or no."

"Yes," came his timid reply.

In a fit of rage, Laura hammered Bruce's chest, sobbing and screaming.

"How could you? How could you do this?"

Stunned by her outburst, he hung his head and left the house.

A torrent of tears punctuated the quiet house as Laura sat by the door waiting for her friend Lisa to pick her up for the luncheon. Lisa's smile quickly dissolved into concern as she saw her friend's state. Clinging to the door for support, Laura fell into Lisa's arms.

"He's having an affair." No matter how often

A gem is not polished without rubbing, nor a man perfected without trials.
—Chinese Proverb

she said the words, she couldn't believe them. Lisa led Laura to a chair and tenderly dried her hair and helped her dress. Laura's tears changed to sniffles until she realized how hopeless things were, and she burst into another crying jag.

Each time Lisa held her and whispered, "Honey, it will be okay." Eventually, Laura's breathing returned to normal, and her tears dried. But she knew life would never be okay.

Together they packed some of Laura's things and drove to Lisa's house.

The agony of removing her wedding ring devastated Laura as she remembered her pledge to always wear the symbol of Bruce's love. Sorrow became Laura's constant companion, her barren hand a constant reminder of her broken heart.

In her anguish Laura prayed for a miracle. *Please God, I'll do whatever you want, but please heal our marriage.* As the weeks passed without the hoped-for miracle, Laura found comfort in sleep. When she wasn't sleeping, attempting to numb the pain, she began drinking heavily, spiraling into an even deeper depression. Her church friends tried to comfort her, but at the end of the day they all returned home to nice, cozy families. How could they comprehend that no amount of comforting would make a difference?

A few months later her friend Patty begged her to go shopping. Without much enthusiasm Laura agreed. She hadn't thought of the old suede purse tossed in the back of the closet for a long time, but it was a comforting reminder. She tossed her wallet, lipstick, and a few other items into the purse before leaving the house to pick up her friend.

While driving and chatting, Laura reached into her purse for a tissue. Feeling a hardness she slowly opened the crumpled tissue. The car began to swerve as Laura cried and laughed at the same time.

"What's the matter? Stay on the road!" Patty watched in amazement as she helped steer the car.

"It's my opal ring!" With shaking hands, Laura slid the prized opal on her vacant, waiting finger.

For the first time in months, Laura felt enveloped in hope as she heard the comforting voice of the Shepherd: "I am betrothed to you forever. Others may desert you, but I am your faithful Bridegroom. I will never abandon you. I have known since the beginning of time when your wounded heart would need this ring as a reassuring symbol of my love. I will never leave you, Laura, never."

On the day she went to court, the Shepherd sent a friend who, while not divorced, understood what Laura must be feeling. That day Laura prayerfully laid at the Shepherd's feet each tear, every feeling of anxiety, apprehension, dread, and exasperation. She clung to His promise that He would never leave her. She believed that the Shepherd would one day do something worthwhile with the horrible situation.

Today, over twenty years later, Laura leads a divorce-recovery ministry and conducts seminars to comfort others going through the devastation of divorce. Laura's heart did not fully mend the day she slipped on the opal ring, but she never forgot the Shepherd's comforting words.

Eventually, the Shepherd healed her broken heart, and his comfort is as real as the opal ring Laura still wears each day.

*And God is able to make all grace abound to you,
so that in all things at all times, having all that you
need, you will abound in every good work.*
—2 Corinthians 9:8

When you come to the bottom, you find God.
—Neville Talbot

'TIS SO SWEET TO TRUST IN JESUS

Louisa M. R. Stead

'Tis so sweet to trust in Jesus,

Just to take Him at His Word;

Just to rest upon His promise,

Just to know, "Thus saith the Lord!"

THE
SHEPHERD WHO
Protects

"YOU PREPARE A TABLE BEFORE ME IN THE PRESENCE OF MY ENEMIES"

OPEN HANDS

Amy couldn't understand why this pregnancy was so different than her previous two. At fifteen weeks, she should have had that glow that everyone raves about when they see a pregnant woman. Instead, her queasy stomach never let her forget the baby she carried. *Other women start feeling better at twelve weeks*, thought the thirty-four-year-old doctor. *I've suffered enough. Just how long is this going to go on?*

Amy had sailed through her first two pregnancies, yet this time, from the very beginning, she knew from her medical training that something wasn't right. Despite her lack of energy, however,

The name of the LORD is a strong tower; the righteous run to it and are safe.
—Proverbs 18:10

Amy pushed herself to care for her family and her patients and even do some community work. The resulting exhaustion made her wonder how she could continue without relief.

Amy's increasingly bad attitude made her snap at her husband, Don, and, whenever possible, to avoid two-year-old Martha Grace and one-year-old Peter. One Sunday in April, her energy depleted, Amy sensed in her heart the Shepherd's answer to how long her suffering might continue. "My child, what if you were to feel this way throughout your entire pregnancy?"

At that moment Amy realized that she had not been living according to Philippians 4:13, "I can do everything through him who gives me strength." She had been trying to do all things through her own strength instead of through God's. "Yes, Lord," she prayed, "if this is what you have for me, I accept it from your hand. Give me grace."

That day Amy's attitude did a complete turn-around. She no longer felt it was her right to feel healthy. She also knew she would have to trust the Shepherd for protection.

Amy didn't know it at the time, but things were about to get worse. Shortly after she turned her pregnancy over to the Shepherd, she felt a big mat of hard, unmoving lymph nodes in her neck. As a doctor, she had felt lymph nodes like that before and knew the diagnosis could be summed up in one word—cancer.

Tiny fissures started in Amy's heart as she sat on the blue recliner watching Don chase their giggling children around the room after their bath. *Thirty minutes ago*, she asked herself with heartbreaking clarity, *would this scene have seemed as immeasurably precious to me as it does now?*

Amy showed the lumps to Don, also a family practitioner, and he said, "Just watch them for a few weeks and see what they do." But Amy knew too much about the human body to let it go. Before turning in, Don examined Amy's neck, and he too began to worry.

That night they held each other as they began to search for answers. Sleep proved elusive for the couple as they discussed what this meant not only to Amy but to their unborn child. Abortion was almost certain to be the advice of most doctors. Amy had long thought that interrupting life before birth was deplorable, but that had only been in theory. Now she had to deal with reality. Could she follow through with her belief even at the cost of her own life? She wrestled through the night and realized that she could never kill the baby she already loved. The Shepherd would just have to protect them both.

The next day Amy and Don prevailed upon their friendship with a surgeon and scheduled an immediate biopsy. Afterwards, Don came to the

If my hands are fully occupied in holding on to something, I can neither give nor receive.

—Dorothee Soelle

recovery room and held Amy's hand. "The frozen section shows Hodgkin's lymphoma."

"Hodgkin's?" Amy said in giddy relief. "That's great. It's treatable."

Later that morning, thanks to the medical literature in the hospital library, Amy and Don learned that Hodgkin's responded to treatment and was often cured. Equally important was Amy's prognosis was the news that most babies exposed to treatment after the first trimester were born healthy if they survived.

The Shepherd had already laid the groundwork for the baby's protection, including Amy's oncologist who happened to be another friend. He guided Amy to a lymphoma specialist who decided on an aggressive chemotherapy regimen. Amy, who had barely taken a Tylenol while pregnant, received her first dose of the toxic chemicals in the beginning of her eighteenth week of gestation. The baby had a one-in-three chance of dying, most likely from the chemotherapy kicking Amy into premature labor. Don and Amy, along with family and friends, prayed for a hedge of protection around both mother and child.

After that first dose, the combination of an empty stomach and Amy's pregnancy caused her to retch repeatedly. But that was only the beginning.

Over the next several months, Amy received seven additional cycles of chemotherapy. Her suffering intensified, and with every bad day came countless fears for her baby. On the days when the nausea lessened, Amy could be optimistic about the baby's future. But when the fatigue and vomiting took over, she fell into the glass-half-empty syndrome: a one-in-three chance of dying. Harder than the physical suffering and more distressing than surrendering her children's care to family and friends was the phrase "one-in-three." Where was the Shepherd's protection? Where was his grace?

Then she read *A Path Through Suffering* by Elisabeth Elliot and found the tool she needed to access the Shepherd's grace. Elliot wrote, "Open hands should characterize the soul's attitude toward God—open to receive what He wants to give, open to give back what He wants to take."

Throughout the pregnancy, Amy remembered Elliot's words and unclasped her grip from her plans, her hopes, and yes, even her baby's life. Five months into chemotherapy, Amy went into premature labor and John was born. Though several weeks early, he weighed over six pounds and was healthy in every way.

The Shepherd not only healed Amy's broken heart the day her son was born, but along the way he protected her through His grace. "God answered our prayers, our hopes, with a yes," Amy says. "But God could just as easily have said no. He would still be a good God. He would have given us the grace to handle it."

That was over ten years ago, and today Amy is cancer free. She has had other disappointments and heartbreaking moments, but she continues to hold her hand open and trust the Shepherd who protects. "He was there through all the suffering, giving me enough strength to get through each day," she says. "None of my strength was left. But God gave me His."

The LORD will keep you from all harm—he will watch over your life; the LORD will watch over your coming and going both now and forevermore.
—Psalm 121:7, 8

This grief, this sorrow, this total loss that empties my hands and breaks my heart, I may, if I will, accept. And by accepting it, I find in my hands something to offer. So I give it back to Him, who in mysterious exchange gives Himself to me.
—Elisabeth Elliot

ROCK OF AGES

AUGUSTUS M. TOPLADY

Rock of Ages, cleft for me,

Let me hide myself in Thee.

Let the water and the blood,

From Thy wounded side which flowed,

Be of sin the double cure;

Save from wrath and make me pure.

CHAPTER TWELVE

THE SHEPHERD WHO

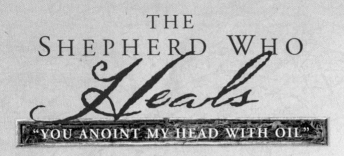

Heals

"YOU ANOINT MY HEAD WITH OIL"

AN ACT OF WILL

One winter afternoon, Ruth came home after an exhaustive session with the tax accountant. For the umpteenth time that month she thought about the life that should have been. This wasn't what she had signed up for when she said, "I do" thirty-five years earlier.

Bill and Ruth were childhood sweethearts in upstate New York, having dated all four years of his navy service and her high-school days. She had just graduated, and Bill was discharged when they pledged their lives to each other. Like other young brides Ruth started her married life convinced that her perfect husband would give her a perfect life.

Teach me to do your will, for you are my God; may your good Spirit lead me on level ground.

—Psalm 143:10

Within five years, Ruth and Bill had four adorable children—two boys and two girls. Eventually, the family relocated to Virginia where Bill got a job with the railroad.

Then in 1984, Bill fell from the top of a moving train and lost both legs. His alcoholism made  his time in the hospital—the trauma unit for three months and thirty days on the regular floor—difficult to watch. After he came home, strange things happened; his hands flew all over, and he had trouble sitting on the commode. He yelled out in the middle of the night. His behavior got uglier everyday and nothing that Ruth did pleased him.

Like so many women of her generation, Ruth had been a stay-at-home mother. She had left the car-and-house maintenance and money matters to Bill. Now everything was her responsibility. She had to learn so many new things, on top of caring for her cantankerous, disabled husband.

I'll just take a short nap before I make dinner, thought Ruth one day after Bill came home from the hospital. A few stressless minutes would help her get through the evening if Bill was in a bad mood. Shortly after Ruth walked into her bedroom, the phone rang. Before she could answer it, she heard her husband murmuring from the other room.

I wonder who's on the phone? Ruth quietly picked up the extension only to hear a woman on the other end.

"Does Steve still live next door?" asked the unidentified voice.

"Yeah," Bill said. "He's the only good kid I have."

Ruth continued to listen as she tried to figure out who Bill was talking to.

"No, you have a daughter right here, and she has turned out really good."

Ruth's hand flew to cover her mouth as she realized what the words she had just heard meant. *It's not possible.* Ruth's ragged breathing slowly calmed as she gently replaced the receiver. *The phone bills,* thought Ruth. After the accident, she had taken over the household bill paying and noticed numerous long-distance phone calls to a New York number she didn't recognize.

Like an out-of-control spinning top, Ruth fell to the bed, her emotions ricocheting from disbelief to fury. *Haven't I been through enough? How can I ever deal with this on top of everything else?*

Crushed and angry, Ruth confronted Bill with her discovery and listened with a sick dread as Bill pieced together the story. His affair with Joyce happened in 1956 while he and Ruth were living in upstate New York. Joyce gave birth to Bill's daughter, Diane. Eventually, Joyce married someone else, and her new husband adopted the baby.

Because Ruth's children were all grown and living on their own, she could leave and start her life over. Out of her pain, she thought about driving

Forgiveness is an act of the will, and the will can function regardless of the temperature of the heart.
—Corrie ten Boom

to New York and confronting this woman. She'd sit in the driveway until the husband came home and boldly walk up to him as he approached his house. She'd show him the phone bills and explain about the affair and the daughter. She'd ruin the other woman's marriage, just like Joyce had ruined Ruth's.

As quickly as she thought of abandoning Bill, she knew she couldn't. Who would take care of him? Bill's drinking had alienated their children, and besides, she didn't want them to become his caregivers.

Ruth began the long process of piecing together her broken heart. For better or worse. Till death do us part. Ruth realized that those weren't empty promises uttered in her fairy-tale wedding. A legless man with an illegitimate daughter was worse than she ever imagined, yet she had no choice but to fulfill the sacred vows.

As Ruth looks back, she says, "I realized the

person that would be hurt the worse by my lack of forgiveness was me. I would be eaten inside like a cancer and turn into a bitter, hateful woman. Even if Bill didn't think he needed me, my children did."

Whenever she felt like the only person who had ever been betrayed, she thought of the Shepherd. He, too, had been betrayed, and yet he had forgiven those same people. Ruth hung onto Proverbs 3:5, 6 during her healing period. As she trusted the Shepherd with all her heart, she began to lean on Him instead of her anger. Once she acknowledged the Shepherd, she knew the right path to take. Slowly, her retaliation plot faded. As her faith in the Shepherd grew, her feelings of revenge lessened.

"I couldn't have survived this alone," Ruth explains, remembering the tearful nights followed by swollen eyes in the morning. "It was a hard lesson for me to learn, but I know that I am a better person, a stronger person because of all that has happened. God's strength carried me along every step of the way."

God's grace has shown Ruth that Bill's daughter, Diane, is not to blame for being born. She facilitated a meeting with Diane and her birth father, and the two women have become friends over the years.

Ruth learned that Martin Luther King, Jr. was right when he said, "Forgiveness does not mean ignoring what has been done or putting a false label on an evil act. It means, rather, that the evil act no longer remains a barrier to the relationship." Thanks to the Shepherd Ruth was able to love her husband again. She took care of him in their home until the end.

The Shepherd not only healed Ruth's heart, but today she can hold her head, up high knowing that as He holds her in His healing arms, she is gradually becoming the woman He designed her to be.

Ruth sums things up like this: "Life rarely plays out the way we anticipate, but it does play out the way God wants it to. And that's all that really matters."

Do not be overcome by evil,
but overcome evil with good.

——Romans 12:21

When deep injury is done us,
we never recover until we forgive.

——Alan Paton

OPEN MY EYES, THAT I MAY SEE

CLARA H. SCOTT

Open my eyes, that I may see

Glimpses of truth Thou hast for me;

Place in my hands the wonderful key

That shall unclasp, and set me free.

CHAPTER THIRTEEN

THE
SHEPHERD OF

ANGEL DOG

From the minute Kelly saw the irrepressible gleam in his black eyes, she knew he was the one. There were others, some more handsome, some in better shape, but somehow Kelly knew this one would always be there for her.

Despite his youthful appearance, he sported a gray muzzle that lessened his chances of being adopted from the humane society. Still, there was something about the stately, black Labrador that made Kelly seek out the volunteer.

"How old is he?"

"Don't be fooled by his premature gray. He's only four and a great pet."

Let us come before him with thanks-giving and extol him with music and song. For the LORD is the great God, the great King above all gods.

—Psalm 95:2, 3

Kelly faced her soon-to-be companion as he stood, not barking or jumping like the dogs in surrounding cages but looking like he, too, felt the immediate bond. Kelly knew that her search was over for a dog to keep her company when her husband was out of town on frequent business. Besides being a buddy, Kelly hoped the large dog would make her feel safe.

"He's a birthday present to me," explained Kelly to her older sister, Kathy, when she told her about the dog she had brought home that March in 1993. "His name is Dallas."

Dallas was Kelly's constant companion and a blessing beyond measure. The large black dog with the gray muzzle became a common sight in the neighborhood. In the winter, to the delight of the children who loved him, Dallas would ride down the snowy hill on the back of the sled with Kelly. When the weather was nice, Kelly and Dallas could often be seen running on the beach they both loved.

Dallas not only kept Kelly company but comforted her when things fell apart at home. Her husband, Jim, was spending more time away, and when he was there, the periods between kind or even civil words grew fewer. His verbal abuse and taunts of Kelly's "shaking all the time" made her miserable, and she turned to Dallas for solace.

Then, in 1997, Jim told Kelly he didn't want to be married anymore. It had been a long time since she had felt loved by Jim, but the news still broke her heart. Even though she'd often spend evenings alone, this was different. Jim wasn't coming back. Kelly sat alone on the sofa where the two had once cuddled. When her tears fell, Dallas put his head in Kelly's lap until she was all cried out. During many nights of crying, mistress and dog gave each other reassurance of their love. If a vicious storm hit, they both slept on the floor to calm each other. Jim might have fallen out of love with Kelly, but Dallas never would.

Two years later, a blood test confirmed the news: the shaking Kelly's ex-husband had ridiculed was in fact one of the first symptoms of Huntington's disease. As hard as the divorce had been, this was infinitely more heartbreaking. Other symptoms

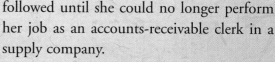

followed until she could no longer perform her job as an accounts-receivable clerk in a supply company.

"Come live with me and Pete," Kathy said when Kelly's job loss meant she couldn't afford the apartment where she and Dallas lived.

"But what about Dallas?"

"He can come him with you," assured Kathy who owned two cats.

Kelly and her beloved Dallas moved in, and the cats, in typical feline fashion, treated the canine with complete indifference. As the disease progressed and Kelly could do less, her friends stopped calling and inviting her to do things with them.

Dallas seemed to sense those days when Kelly felt abandoned, and he would nuzzle her with his gray beard and tell her with his deep, soulful eyes that he was her friend.

The best thing about Dallas was that he was so *there*. His unconditional love withstood Kelly's irritability and other personality changes that were the result of her neurological disease. Nothing mattered to Dallas; she was still his Kelly. His worry and concern always buoyed Kelly's spirit. Kelly knew Dallas was her guardian angel sent to her to help her through difficult times.

As Dallas suffered a slow decline in his health and became more fragile with age, Kathy and Pete wondered what to do. Eventually, they decided to get a puppy while Dallas was still with them. Dallas was irreplaceable, so they knew another black Labrador was out of the question. Instead, they settled on Moose, a ten-week-old cairn terrier. Rather like an elder statesman, the sedate Dallas

Those who loved you and were helped by you will remember you. So carve your name on hearts and not on marble.
—C. H. Spurgeon

allowed Moose more latitude than one would have thought possible. The two dogs became good friends, in part because Dallas allowed the frisky puppy to crawl all over him and bite him.

Two months after Moose moved in, almost as if Dallas knew that his new friend was ready to take over, the older dog's condition worsened. Each step proved more difficult than the day before, and he could barely stand up to walk.

"Look at Dallas," Kelly said to Kathy one day that last February. "It's cold outside. He needs to come in." But once outside, it was too much for the shorthaired dog to come back in without excruciating pain.

Like people, dogs are not immortal and, despite Kelly's prayers to the Shepherd, it was obvious to everyone that Dallas could not go on. That week Dallas slept out in the yard, oblivious to the biting cold, barely responding. On his last day in the backyard, Dallas was unable to stand.

"Kathy, he's in so much pain," said Kelly barely holding back her tears as she saw the anguish in her best friend's eyes. "I can't let him suffer anymore."

With the Shepherd's help, Kelly walked out to the yard, and along with Pete, picked Dallas up and carried him to the car. All the way to the veterinarian's office, Kelly cried and thanked the Shepherd for bringing such a blessing into her life. How could she have survived divorce and disease without Dallas?

Kelly held Dallas as the vet put him to sleep. She felt the same as when Helen Keller said, "With every friend I love who has been taken into the brown bosom of the earth, a part of me has been buried there; but their contribution to my being of happiness, strength and understanding remains to sustain me in an altered world."

I like to think that God's sovereign choices in this world include the pairing of pets and people.

In this case, the Shepherd, knowing that a brave woman would need a sweet, patient dog, sent Dallas to Kelly. Dallas lives in Kelly's heart, and his ashes and pictures sit on her dresser. Because the neurological disease continues to destroy her

brain, Kelly's world is being altered in ways she has yet to understand. Her grieving has been more intense because of her illness, but so was her love for her angel dog, the Shepherd's blessing, in her life.

Though he brings grief, he will show compassion, so great is his unfailing love.
—Lamentations 3:32

We give them the love we can spare, the time we can spare. In return dogs have given us their absolute all. It is without doubt the best deal man has ever made.
—Roger Caras

O THOU FROM WHOM ALL GOODNESS FLOWS

THOMAS HAWEIS

O Thou, from Whom all goodness flows,

I lift my heart to Thee;

In all my sorrows, conflicts, woes,

Dear Lord, remember me.

THE SHEPHERD WHO

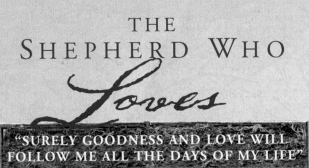

Loves

"SURELY GOODNESS AND LOVE WILL FOLLOW ME ALL THE DAYS OF MY LIFE"

I LOVE YOU, DADDY

It was unusual that Charlie was in Florida in January. He lived in San Antonio, Texas, but made the trek to see my 48-year-old husband once a year for David's September birthday. Now here it was, only five months since my father-in-law's last trip, and Charlie was not only visiting Florida but the nursing home as well.

When David was initially diagnosed with a rare neurological disease, Charlie refused to believe it had no cure. The first year he decided that playing an instrument would give David's brain exercise. He offered to buy an organ, but because of the size

I will be glad and rejoice in your love, for you saw my affliction and knew the anguish of my soul.
—Psalm 31:7

and expense, I suggested a compromise, and an electronic keyboard arrived. David never touched it.

Next came the ancient electric bicycle Charlie delivered on one of his rare visits. David rode it for a while with no outward change except the pool of grease on our lanai floor. Articles and books arrived from Charlie, along with advice, but David's condition worsened.

Charlie's barrage of information and suggestions seemed like a criticism of the care I was giving his son. With 20/20 hindsight I now realize that Charlie was trying to piece together his shattered heart.

I cannot imagine watching my child go through the mental, psychological, and physical symptoms that make up Huntington's disease. No matter how old, how tall, how much grief they cause me, my sons are still my babies and always will be. I know that's how Charlie felt, too.

David loved movies, and despite his traitorous

body and his inability to do anything for himself, he enjoyed our frequent outings to the local theater. What a surprise I got when I walked in to get David for our Friday date. Charlie stood talking to David's aide by the nurse's station. Charlie, who refused to accept that his son needed to be in the nursing home, was there with him.

"Charlie! What are you doing here?"

"Just wanted to congratulate David for making it to the year 2000," he replied. "This is a big occasion."

With no warning, he had flown in from Texas to be with David and tour the facility. We talked in the car on the way back to Island Lake after seeing the movie *Snow Falling on Cedar*. Well, Charlie and I talked. David's speech had gone from difficult to garbled and was now almost non-existent. Despite being able to understand what was going on around him, I had not heard him make more than a few sounds in over six months.

"I need to go back to the car and change my hearing-aid batteries," Charlie explained before he walked out of the room once we settled David into his wheelchair. "I won't be long."

An idea came to me as Charlie went to the car. "David, we need to practice while your dad is gone," I pleaded. "Please, David. Say, 'I love you, Dad.' I know you can do it."

David stared at me intently as he worked his mouth. Meaningless sounds came out, but not the words I knew his father so wanted to hear.

"David, I know you can do this. After you say this, you never have to talk again if you don't want to, but please, try as hard as you can. Please?"

With intensity, David tried to say the few words that would warm Charlie's heart, but each time he got to the word "love" it fell apart. It was just too hard. After several tries, I gave up. Charlie would just have to know in his heart that David loved him.

"That's better," said Charlie as he reentered the room. "Now I can hear anything important."

David began to shift in his chair and flail his arms.

"Did you want to say something, David?" I prompted.

I knew that despite all the changes from Huntington's, David was still in there trying desperately to get out. I held my breath and smiled my encouragement.

With great effort, David slowly but clearly said the four words that I know Charlie heard over and over on his way back to Texas. He broke into a grin as he triumphantly declared, "I love you, Daddy!"

As Charlie knelt to hug David in his wheelchair, he buried his face in his son's shoulder. The tears he shed were tears of joy from hearing his son proclaim his love.

Love doesn't make the world go round. Love is what makes the ride worthwhile.
—Franklin P. Jones

David never spoke again and Charlie never made another September birthday trek. He died unexpectedly of an aneurysm three weeks after he hugged his son.

In her book, *Death Comes for the Archbishop*, Willa Cather said, "Where there is great love, there are always miracles." The Shepherd of miracles was also in the room the day that, against all odds, David told his father he loved him.

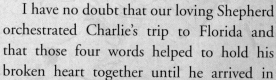

I have no doubt that our loving Shepherd orchestrated Charlie's trip to Florida and that those four words helped to hold his broken heart together until he arrived in heaven. Charlie had no way of knowing that he would never again see his son on this earth, but they are finally together in heaven now. I have this picture of Charlie with the Shepherd close by, no hearing aid needed, hearing David say to him, "I love you, Daddy."

I trust in your unfailing love.
—Psalm 13:5

Love can achieve unexpected majesty
in the rocky soil of misfortune.
—Tony Snow

O LOVE THAT WILT NOT LET ME GO

GEORGE MATHESON

O Love that wilt not let me go,

I rest my weary soul in thee.

I give Thee back the life I owe,

That in Thine ocean depths its flow

May richer, fuller be.

CHAPTER FIFTEEN

THE SHEPHERD OF

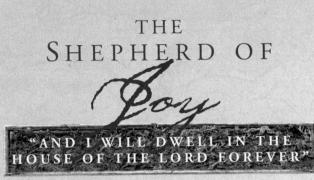

"AND I WILL DWELL IN THE HOUSE OF THE LORD FOREVER"

I'M GONNA' BELIEVE

"Lord, give me something to get through the dishes," said a bored and lonely Nancy one fall evening in 1993. With her hands in the soapy water, she composed what later became an international hit. The first line of the peppy, upbeat song, "I'm gonna' believe that you are up to something good," cheered Nancy and in no time the dishes were washed and dried and the song complete.

Later, Nancy's husband, J.R., and their friends, Ruth and Victor, Mexican missionaries staying with them, came in from a missions conference. Enchanted with the lighthearted tune, Ruth imme-

No eye has seen, no ear has heard, no mind has conceived what God has prepared for those who love him.

—1 Corinthians 2:9

diately translated it into Spanish. Ruth and Victor returned to Mexico and they brought the song to their denomination. "Up to Something Good" soon became a favorite, and now, when Nancy goes to one of their churches in Latin America, she is introduced as the lady who wrote "Yo Voy A Creer," which is Spanish for "I'm going to believe."

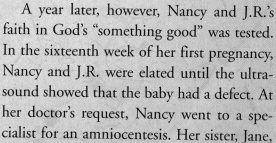

A year later, however, Nancy and J.R.'s faith in God's "something good" was tested. In the sixteenth week of her first pregnancy, Nancy and J.R. were elated until the ultrasound showed that the baby had a defect. At her doctor's request, Nancy went to a specialist for an amniocentesis. Her sister, Jane, who had lost a full-term son to stillbirth a couple of years earlier, met Nancy at the hospital and held her hand during the procedure.

The heartbreaking news that their little boy carried a triple eighteenth chromosome—a condition called trisomy 18—was devastating.

"You don't have to go through this," said the specialist when she recommended Nancy have an abortion. "This is a fatal condition," she reminded her before leaving the room.

"I felt like a truck ran over me after spending time with her," says Nancy describing the appointment. While the doctor was clinical in her attitude, her nurse, a compassionate Christian, talked to Nancy after the doctor left, and she gave Nancy a book called, *When Hello Means Good-bye*. The book was the Shepherd's way of helping Nancy and J.R. come to terms with what they were facing and to make plans for what they would do if and when their son died.

Abortion was never a consideration for the baby they decided to name John Richard III. They wanted this baby for as long as God would allow, whatever his condition.

A few days after they learned about little J. R.'s condition their phone rang.

"I had the strongest feeling I should call you. What's going on?" asked Ruth who had been at Nancy's house a year earlier.

Ruth listened to Nancy pour out her heart but didn't say a word. Instead, she sang the words Nancy had composed the previous year over her kitchen sink.

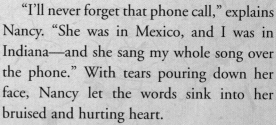

"I'll never forget that phone call," explains Nancy. "She was in Mexico, and I was in Indiana—and she sang my whole song over the phone." With tears pouring down her face, Nancy let the words sink into her bruised and hurting heart.

"J. R. and I held on to that song for the rest of the pregnancy," Nancy continues. "It was an anchor to our faith. We couldn't understand why we were going through this, but we knew Jesus, and we could believe that he was good, and he was doing good things in our lives."

Over the next months, people throughout the

United States, Mexico, and other countries where J.R. and Nancy had ministered prayed to the Shepherd on their behalf. Despite their anguish, the prayers lifted and carried them through the unthinkable. "We cried, struggled, and had the peace of the Lord all at the same time," Nancy said. "It was both the most difficult and the most beautiful experience we ever had."

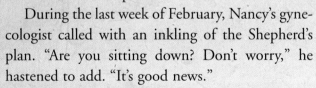

Despite his negative prognosis and the warning that he could be stillborn, little J.R. continued to grow and kick. Trusting the Shepherd, they prepared a nursery so they'd be ready if he were actually able to come home from the hospital.

During the last week of February, Nancy's gynecologist called with an inkling of the Shepherd's plan. "Are you sitting down? Don't worry," he hastened to add. "It's good news."

The doctor explained that the patient of one of the doctors in his group was pregnant. "She needs to place the baby for adoption and wants to be sure it goes to a Christian home. Are you interested? The baby will be born about three months after yours."

After praying, Nancy and J.R. chose to believe that God was indeed up to something good. They told the doctor they would love to have the baby.

In her eighth month, Nancy's blood pressure began to rise to the point where a Caesarean was needed. Knowing the great likelihood that they would be saying good-bye to little J.R. made setting the date for the operation difficult.

On Friday night, March 10, 1995, around 7:30 p.m., the doctor delivered little J.R. by C-section. He lived for two hours with the help of a breathing tube. J.R. cradled the baby for the first hour while Nancy came out of the anesthesia. Once she was fully awake, Nancy held her precious son. "He opened up his eyes and looked at me. I felt like he was saying, 'I did the best I could, Mom!'"

One joy shatters a hundred griefs.
—Chinese Proverb

Wearing sterile gowns, family and friends went into the neonatal intensive-care room by twos to see the tableau. Nancy and J.R. had agreed with the doctor that the breathing tube would be removed after two hours. It was the Shepherd's providence that J.R.'s brother, an inhalation thera-pist, was the one to remove the tube. With a full heart, J.R. cradled his son as the baby went to be with the Shepherd.

After the nurses had taken his foot and handprints, Nancy and J.R. gave little J.R. a bath, dressed him in a special outfit, and looked him over from head to toe. "I espe-cially loved the feel of his skin just behind the knees—so soft," Nancy says.

Despite their grief, Nancy and J.R. had the anticipation of joy for the next three months as they prayed about adopting the promised baby. Rather than letting her milk dry up naturally, Nancy asked if she could breastfeed the adopted baby.

"Oh, that's too much trouble," came the response. "Just recover from surgery, and feed the baby formula." But Nancy wasn't satisfied with that. "I pumped my milk for three months, freezing some of the milk in sterile bags, which we called baby Popsicles. There was so much," she laughingly remembers, "I had to ask friends to store it in their freezers."

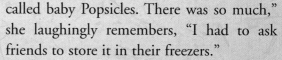

When they learned their new baby was a boy they named him William after Nancy's father. The birth mother had a C-section and made arrangements for the couple to go into the newborn nursery as soon as the baby was delivered. They were with William when he was twenty minutes old and he nursed during that first hour. "It was so amazing to return to the same hospital where we had lost little J.R. and receive William. The doctors and nurses rejoiced with us."

At one point in their journey so many people around the world were praying that Nancy thought, "Lord, you're going to have to heal this baby just to protect your reputation." She needn't have worried because the Shepherd was not only up to something good but something joyful. Nancy and J.R. now have two sons, one waiting for them in heaven and one a championship baseball player. They know that one day their family will be together in everlasting joy.

The Shepherd was up to something good for William and Nancy and J.R. They needed each other, and the Lord brought them together. "Now I know through experience that I can trust the Lord when things look their worst," says Nancy. "He is a redeemer, an expert at taking something terrible and making something beautiful out of it." Truly, He is the Shepherd of joy.

When anxiety was great within me, your consolation
brought joy to my soul.
—Psalm 94:19

We enjoy warmth because we have been cold.
We appreciate light because we have been in
darkness. By the same token, we can experience
joy because we have known sorrow.
—David L. Weatherford

TO GOD BE THE GLORY

FANNY CROSBY

Praise the Lord, praise the Lord,

Let the earth hear His voice!

Praise the Lord, praise the Lord,

Let the people rejoice!

O come to the Father, thro' Jesus, the Son,

And give Him the glory—great things He hath done.

I'm gonna believe
That you are up to something good
I'm gonna believe
That you are up to something good
When I can't understand
The things that happen in my life
I'm gonna believe
That you are up to something good

"I'll never fail or forsake you"
That is what you said
"Through fire and water I will take you"
That is what you said
So when you don't answer my prayer
The way I think you should
I'm gonna believe
That you are up to something good

Nancy Honeytree Miller

Let your tears come. Let them water your soul.
—Eileen Mayhew

Carmen Leal has experienced firsthand the comfort that only the Shepherd can bring during times of brokenness. She is the author and creator of the Twenty-Third series including *The Twenty-Third Psalm for Caregivers*, *The Twenty-Third Psalm for Those Who Grieve*, and *The Twenty-Third Psalm for Single Parents*. A storyteller who has a dramatic testimony, she is a popular presenter at women's retreats, church groups, conventions, and conferences.

To have Carmen speak to your group, please visit **http://www.thetwentythirdpsalm.com**

*Thank you to those who graciously shared
private details of your lives that others might
see how the Shepherd restored your souls.
Your stories give others hope.*

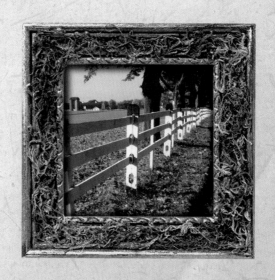

If it were

not for hopes

the heart

would

break.

— *Thomas Fuller*